bs 17/0<

Prentice Hall Guides
To Advanced Communication

Guide to
Report Writing

Michael Netzley
Carlson School of Management
University of Minnesota

Craig Snow
School of Hotel Administration
Cornell University

156187X

PRENTICE HALL
Upper Saddle River, New Jersey 07458

For S.V.U., whose patience and support helped me complete this project. – M.N.
To Lisa, Lee, Michael, Raffi, and S.J. – C.S.

Library of Congress Cataloging-in-Publication Data

Netzley, Michael.
    Guide to report writing / Michael Netzley, Craig Snow.
        p. cm. — (The Prentice-Hall guides to advanced business communication)
    ISBN 0-13-041771-8
    1. English language—Business English.   2. Business report writing.   3. Business writing.
    4. Report writing.   I. Snow, Craig. II. Title. III. Series.

PE1479.B87 N48   2001
808′.06665—dc21   2001021997

VP/Editor-in-Chief: Jeff Shelstad
Assistant Editor: Jennifer Surich
Editorial Assistant: Virginia Sheridan
Media Project Manager:
    Michele Faranda
Senior Marketing Manager:
    Debbie Clare
Marketing Assistant: Brian Rappelfeld
Managing Editor (Production):
    Judy Leale
Production Editor: Theresa Festa
Production Assistant: Keri Jean
Permissions Coordinator:
    Suzanne Grappi
Associate Director, Manufacturing:
    Vincent Scelta

Production Manager:
    Arnold Vila
Design Manager: Patricia Smythe
Designer: Steve Frim
Art Director: Jayne Conte
Cover Design: Kiwi Design
Associate Director, Multimedia
    Production: Karen Goldsmith
Manager, Print Production:
    Christy Mahon
Composition: Rainbow Graphics
Full-Service Project Management:
    Rainbow Graphics
Printer/Binder:
    Victor Graphics, Inc.

Credits and acknowledgements borrowed from other sources and reproduced, with permission, in this textbook appear on appropriate page within text.

Prentice
    Hall

10 9 8 7 6 5
ISBN 0-13-041771-8

Table of Contents

CHAPTER I

WHAT MAKES REPORTS EFFECTIVE

CHAPTER 2

HOW TO MANAGE THE REPORT-WRITING PROCESS

CHAPTER 3

WHAT KEY ELEMENTS TO INCLUDE IN A REPORT

CHAPTER 4

HOW TO DESIGN A READABLE REPORT

APPENDIX

Introduction

HOW THIS BOOK CAN HELP YOU

This book will help you to write user-friendly reports. If you are among those professionals who rely on reports for communicating—or receiving—important information, then this book can help you to:

- Establish and maintain your credibility as a professional.
- Understand what effective reports are and how to create them.
- Plan and execute your projects so that you use your time wisely and efficiently.
- Identify and gather the information you need, analyze it appropriately, and shape it so that you accomplish your project goals.
- Design reports that are inviting, attractive, and readable.
- Create reports that get read and understood—and that convey data, conclusions, and recommendations that get accepted and acted upon.

Once you understand the essential report features, as well as the key principles that underlie the preparation and writing of reports, you will be able to make informed choices that will enable you to create virtually any report: of any length, for any purposes, for any audiences, in any field. For as we hope to demonstrate in the pages that follow, a report (to paraphrase Gertrude Stein) is a report is a report. That is, although actual reports may differ in a variety of ways—among them, length, dress, type of information they contain, purpose, and more—in the essential elements they are similar.

If you would like information about other kinds of communication in a business or management setting, please see the other books in this Prentice Hall series in Advanced Communication. All of the books in this series are short, professional, and readable.

- *Guide to Electronic Communication* by Kristen DeTienne (Prentice Hall, 2002)
- *Guide to Managerial Communication: Effective Business Writing and Speaking* by Mary Munter (Prentice Hall, 2000)
- *Guide to Meetings* by Mary Munter and Michael Netzley (Prentice Hall, 2002)
- *Guide to Presentations* by Mary Munter and Lynn Russell (Prentice Hall, 2002)

WHO CAN USE THIS BOOK

If you are interested in the success of your organization and are committed to your own professional growth—as well as the professional growth of your colleagues—then you should find value in this book. You should find this book especially useful if you are an MBA-level student who writes reports for any of your courses, a business professional who writes reports, a manager or executive whose staff writes reports for you to read, or a consultant.

- *MBA students:* This book is designed to be used as a core text in an MBA-level managerial communications course or as a supplementary text for virtually any MBA-level course that calls for students to create and deliver reports in any function area: finance, marketing, organizational behavior, operations management, technology, consulting, and more.

- *Business professionals:* This book is designed to meet the needs of business professionals—in any field—whose success in the workplace depends, at least in part, on their ability to solve problems and communicate their solutions effectively.

- *Managers or executives:* This book can help managers or executives who frequently read reports by enhancing their ability to guide fellow employees—subordinates and teammates—as they prepare reports.

- *Consultants:* This book should deliver special value for those involved in consulting, whether they are internal or external consultants, working independently or for a large domestic or international consulting firm. The quality of the consulting solutions they deliver to their clients depends in no small part on the quality of reports with which they communicate those solutions.

WHY THIS BOOK WAS WRITTEN

The thousands of participants in various professional report-writing courses and workshops we have taught—between the two of us, at Cornell University, University of Minnesota, Purdue University, Miami University, Iowa State University, Albion College, and Washington University's John M. Olin School of Business, as well as at dozens of companies and organizations—tell us they want a brief summary of report writing techniques. Such busy professionals have found other books on this subject too long or too remedial for their needs. That's why Prentice Hall is publishing this series, the Prentice Hall Guides to Advanced Communication—brief, practical, reader-friendly guides for people who communicate in professional contexts. (See the inside front cover of this book for more information on the series.)

- *Brief:* The book summarizes key ideas only. Culling from thousands of pages of text and research, we have omitted bulky examples, cases, footnotes, exercises, and discussion questions.

- *Practical:* This book offers clear, straightforward tools you can use. It includes only information you will find useful in a professional context.

- *Reader-friendly:* We have tried to provide an easy-to-skim format—using a direct, matter-of-fact, and nontheoretical tone.

HOW THIS BOOK IS ORGANIZED

This book is organized into five main sections.

Chapter 1 explains what makes reports effective—by identifying what reports are, how they are used, and what key virtues they share.

Chapter 2 explains how you can manage your report-writing process effectively—by describing what you should consider as you plan and execute your projects.

Chapter 3 explains the components of an effective report—by identifying the key elements to include.

Chapter 4 explains what you can do to design readable reports—by identifying how you can enhance the clarity and skim-value of your report.

And the appendix guides you through a formal report's front-end materials—by providing illustrations of a letter of transmittal, executive summary, title page, and table of contents.

ACKNOWLEDGMENTS

We acknowledge the many people who helped us make this book possible.

M.N. I would like to thank Carolyn Boulger, Mary Munter, and JoAnn Syverson for all their help, guidance, and patience with this project. Their willingness to support, respond, and provide feedback was invaluable. I would also like to thank Craig and Mary for their time, energy, and commitment to this project.

C.S. If it is true that the key to growth entails surrounding yourself with people who will hold you to high standards, then I have been multiply blessed. First, I have been blessed with an immediate family and close friends who have long maintained high expectations. Second, I benefited from the example and encouragement of Leonora Woodman, under whose tutelage I first leaned to teach; and from Jeanne Halpern, who, as mentor to a generation of students at Purdue University, inspired us and helped us to raise our standards of professionalism. Third, I had the good fortune to work with the talented MBA students, faculty, and administration at Washington University's John M. Olin School of Business, 1995–1998, who persuaded me, despite my reluctance, to add to the world's bookshelves on managerial communication. And fourth, I found great pleasure in working with Michael and Mary, who provided the right blend of encouragement and intellectual stimulation to push our collective thinking and, I hope, capture this moment of truth.

Michael Netzley
Carlson School of Management
University of Minnesota

Craig Snow
School of Hotel Administration
Cornell University

CHAPTER I OUTLINE

I. WHAT REPORTS ARE
   1. Reports may take different forms
   2. Reports include a collection of data
   3. Reports are adapted for their readers

II. HOW REPORTS ARE USED
   1. Periodic reports to learn about recent activities
   2. Special-project reports to make informed decisions

III. WHAT VIRTUES EFFECTIVE REPORTS SHARE
   1. Content value
   2. Skim value
   3. Clarity

CHAPTER I

What Makes Reports Effective

If you devote just a few minutes surfing the web, reviewing written messages from business or government agencies, or even glancing at the daily newspaper, you will find regular references to reports. Reports frequently serve as the basis for what journalists present as news, especially business news. Reports may well be the chief vehicle by which organizations—from the worlds of business, government, and the nonprofit sector—communicate authoritative and substantive news: the results of investigations, the latest earnings, periodic sales figures, and more.

Reports also serve a major function within many organizations— where individuals, teams, task forces, committees, and the like need to communicate authoritative and reliable information to key constituencies. Reports are not limited by field or industry; they are used in all kinds of organizations.

Although reports typically emerge from organizations, people like you within organizations prepare reports. And reports are likely to be among the most important messages you will prepare at work. The quality of your reports will likely influence your professional success, perhaps even more so than the quality of the other workplace messages you create and deliver. For the reports that you create depict your competence: how well you think; how well you gather, assemble, and analyze data; how well you draw conclusions and recommendations from data; how well you support your assertions; and how well you create messages that meet the needs of your readers. Your credibility, then, is on the line every time you prepare a report.

To help you prepare these important and often complex messages, this chapter covers what reports are, how they are used, and what their chief virtues are.

I. WHAT REPORTS ARE

Reports, put simply, are messages that present a collection of data thoughtfully adapted to the needs of the report readers—to help them make informed decisions within a professional context. People write reports because they need to or choose to transmit information that will help accomplish specific professional goals. Effective reports enable the writers to accomplish specific business goals as they inform, persuade, or both. More specifically, reports (1) may take different forms, (2) include a collection of data, and (3) are adapted to their readers.

1. Reports may take different forms.

Reports may be presented in a host of shapes and sizes: varying in length, content, format, visual design, function, level of development, style, and other ways. No matter how they may differ, though, most reports are similar in that they present data to help audiences make informed decisions within professional contexts.

Many variables may be isolated as distinguishing features that help you to classify reports. However, most of these variables overlap when applied to reports. Consider the following ways that reports may be classified. These bases for classifying reports may well help you to make appropriate choices as you plan your own reports.

By length   Reports may be classified as short or long, relative to the norms within a particular organization (e.g., one to nine pages for a short report; ten pages or more for a long report).

By content   Some reports are strictly numerical, while others may provide detailed prose discussion that includes conclusions and/or recommendations.

By format or "dress"   Some reports may be presented in a simple, conventional memo format (with a traditional memo heading followed by the prose message), while others may be dressed more formally (with a separate title page, transmittal message, table of contents, list of figures, stand-alone executive summary, extensive prose discussion, and appendices).

By function or stage in the problem-solving process Reports may be classified as proposals (which lay out the plans for a study, project, initiative, or course of action), progress reviews (which provide periodic updates on the status of an activity), and completion reports (which communicate the solution or results—that is, data, conclusions, and/or recommendations—at the close of a project).

By frequency Reports may be classified as periodic (i.e., routine) or as special-project (i.e., nonroutine).

* *Periodic:* Depending on the needs of the organization that produces them, periodic reports may be prepared daily, weekly, biweekly, monthly, quarterly, semiannually, annually, or according to some other frequency. Sales reports, for instance, are relatively common routine reports in which individual salespeople, departments, or even individual divisions of a multi-unit company present sales results for a given period. Annual reports, similarly, are important periodic reports that many organizations produce.

* *Special-project:* Special-project reports, in contrast, are prepared to meet specific needs for writers and readers. People who conduct studies often prepare special-project reports as they proceed through their investigation. These special-project reports encompass a broad category of messages that vary depending on their unique function as they guide readers through a particular stage in a multiple-stage process. Among the most common of these reports are proposals, progress reviews, and completion reports.

2. Reports include a collection of data.

Reports are typically data driven. The data may emerge from primary or secondary sources, with either extensive or minimal research. The data may be based on experiments, surveys, company records, interviews, focus groups, direct observation, or even personal experience. The data may be statistical, empirical, textual, visual, or some combination. Regardless of the nature and amount of data that a report presents, top-quality report writers provide a service to their readers by thoughtfully selecting and synthesizing report data.

Selecting   Effective data collection for reports is guided by three criteria:

- *Content quality:* Does the message present useful information in the form of data, conclusions, and/or recommendations from the data?

- *Reliability:* Is the data—the specific evidence that constitutes the raw material of reports—reliable? Is the data verifiable and accurate? Are any conclusions and recommendations that the report presents supported by sound evidence and reasoning?

- *Self-sufficiency:* Does the message present enough data and explanation so that the target audience can use the report, without additional discussion, to make informed decisions?

Synthesizing   The data in effective reports is then synthesized—generalized, grouped, and sequenced to meet reader needs.

- *Generalizing:* The data may be presented with or without interpretation (the conclusions and/or recommendations that result from analysis of the data).

- *Grouping:* The data, as well as any corresponding conclusions and recommendations, are grouped into segment topics according to some organizing principle.

- *Sequencing:* The segment topics are arranged according to a logical and suitable sequencing principle. Consider the following alternatives:

    By degree: Most to least important, largest to smallest, most to least recommended—or vice versa

    By chronology: Most to least recent, least to most recent, or steps in a process

    By function: Component parts (of a whole), strengths and weaknesses, or points of agreement and disagreement

    By audience questions (implicit or explicit): What to do, why to do it, where to begin? Or what it is, how it benefits you, what it costs and entails?

EXPLODING REPORT MYTHS	
Myth	**Truth**
Reports are entirely different from memos and letters.	Reports may be formatted as memos or letters.
Reports are strictly "objective" presentation of factual data.	Report writers use their best judgment to select data to provide in reports.
Reports are mere collections of data: They should not incorporate the writer's opinion.	Reports should be adapted to the needs of the readers. • If readers merely need numerical or factual data, then mere numerical or factual data should be sufficient. • If readers rely on the report writer to interpret the data, then the report should incorporate the writer's best attempt to draw conclusions and, if appropriate, recommendations.
A report should be structured as a sequence of steps in which the writer engaged in the "discovery process" to collect the data.	A report should be structured according to the needs of the readers: to learn conclusions or to act on recommendations.

3. Reports are adapted for their readers.

Effective reports meet the needs and expectations of the report readers. As you compose your reports, you should adapt to the needs of your key readers: those who will use your reports to make informed decisions, as well as those who will be most affected by the decisions that your report influences. Reports are composed because of a specific need somewhere in an organization; therefore, each report should help one or more people within that organization solve some problem.

Understand how readers approach reports   Report readers are task oriented: they read reports so that they may understand and, where appropriate, act. Workplace readers do not read reports as they might read an essay or a literary work—leisure or pastime reading that might entertain or enchant the reader via literary devices such as intriguing plot, characterization, imagery, or metaphor. Similarly, workplace readers do not use reports to learn about routine workplace activities such as meeting notices, lunch date arrangements, or scheduling changes.

An effective report is not a random collection of data, not a mind dump, nor an opinion piece designed for a reader at leisure. An effective report, instead, is a well-structured message that is designed to be read quickly and help readers understand and act on information. Effective reports are functional tools that help people—managers, executives, lawyers, doctors, government administrators, and countless others—make informed decisions. Effective reports, further, are timely: They arrive when promised and present current information.

Adapt to the needs of your key readers   Adapting to all the needs of all potential report audiences might be impractical. All potential readers of a particular report might include specialists in your field, colleagues within your organizations, laypeople, journalists, lawyers, government regulators, and more. If you were to try to adapt to all the needs of this diverse group of potential readers, you might find yourself creating excessively long and detailed reports that meet the needs of few, if any, actual readers—especially the distinct individual or group of readers for whom you have most specifically prepared the report.

Instead of trying to design reports that would address all needs of all possible readers, then, you need to be selective about which readers to adapt to. That is, you need to identify those readers most likely to be affected by your report. Who will be the readers most likely to read it—or to use the information it contains? Who will be the readers most likely to make decisions based on the information within the report? And what decisions will they use the report to make? By considering these questions, you can identify your key readers; adapt to their needs as you make informed choices concerning the topics, level of development, and structure of your report; and thereby enable your key readers to use each report you compose.

II. HOW REPORTS ARE USED

Because report readers use reports to obtain information for a variety of purposes unique to each situation—i.e., each organization, specific job, and function—reports will often vary from organization to organization. Nevertheless, most reports are similar in that readers use reports to learn about activities and to make informed decisions. All reports should be designed to enable readers to secure either or both of these goals.

I. Periodic reports to learn about recent activities

Some reports serve as a record of events for those audiences who want to learn about recent activities within organizations. For example, the regional manager of a chain of retail clothing stores may want to learn daily, weekly, and monthly sales figures from each store. Individual investors expect their investment management companies to provide them with reports on their portfolios. Government administrators may solicit a report from an organization to determine whether the organization has complied with equal employment opportunity hiring regulations.

Reports that document recent activities are typically referred to as *periodic reports*. These reports collect and transmit data: daily, weekly, monthly, semiannually, annually, or according to some other periodic need of the report audiences. Occasionally, these reports may be routine collections of data, but these reports can also be long, detailed, and complex. Following are common periodic reports that businesses use.

Sales reports   Sales professionals regularly report sales achievements to their managers. Within retail sales companies, hotels, or restaurants, for instance, managers regularly review sales figures so that they can determine how well the company, department, product line, or even individual sales agent is performing. Depending on the organization, these reports may be produced daily, weekly, biweekly, monthly, or quarterly.

- *Focus on data:* Many sales reports focus exclusively on data: units sold, price, etc.

  Example: Well-managed food-service outlets will keep track of and report on features such as how many burgers were sold in a given time period, what items sold with them, what each item cost, and what times of day were most and least productive.

  Example: Consumer-products manufacturers track the types and number of items produced, as well as the purchasers for each item: for each stock-keeping unit, well-managed companies maintain current and accurate information.

- *Focus on recommendations:* Other sales reports may include conclusions and recommendations: to explain and identify ways to improve sales performance.

  Example: Regional managers for multi-unit apparel stores, for instance, may use sales figures from one region, where sales may be especially high, as a basis for determining and communicating initiatives to raise sales in another region.

Financial reports   Businesses report key financial data periodically (e.g., monthly, quarterly, annually): to the government, the press, the investment community, stockholders, and others. Here are some examples.

- *Quarterly financial reports*

  Example: Earnings reports are common periodic financial reports. Companies whose stock is publicly traded are required to report their financial results quarterly. The Securities and Exchange Commission uses these reports to monitor compliance with federal guidelines, and the investment community uses these reports to make investment decisions and recommendations.

  Example: Investment statements are a type of periodic financial report. Investment companies, on a quarterly (or occasionally monthly) basis, will report to their clients the status of their accounts. This information—usually presented as mere data, without conclusions or recommendations—will typically be organized as follows to meet the needs of the clients: by total holdings, by comparison with the preceding period, and by individual account holdings and activity.

- *Monthly financial reports*

  Example: Monthly bank statements are another type of periodic financial report. Banks use these messages to report to their customers the status of their accounts.

  Example: Monthly bills that companies send to their customers are a type of financial report. For instance, an electric bill would include a usage report (e.g., kilowatt hours used during a particular period) that would likely include a comparison with similar periods, as well as an explanation of charges for the period in question.

Annual reports   Many organizations create and disseminate annual reports to communicate with their key constituencies (e.g., current and potential investors, governmental regulatory agencies, current and prospective employees, and the news media). These periodic reports (like semiannual and quarterly reports) present audiences with news: how the organization has performed during the period in question, what have been the key achievements, and perhaps even what the future prospects are.

Personnel evaluations   Among the most important reports for workers in many organizations is the personnel evaluation, or performance review. In some organizations, new employees are hired on a probationary status and then reviewed after a predetermined period; during and after that period, their performance is reviewed and documented in their personnel file. In many organizations, even veteran employees are reviewed periodically (e.g., semiannually or annually); the results of these reviews are documented in personnel files.

Minutes   Formal committees within organizations typically report on their activities via minutes, which document what took place during committee meetings—what topics were addressed, what key points were raised, and what actions were agreed on.

2. Special-project reports to make informed decisions

For some audiences who want to decide on a course of action, reports provide them with the information that may serve as the basis for managerial decisions. Rather than make important decisions in an information vacuum, managers rely on reports that present concrete data, as well as corresponding conclusions and recommendations.

Aside from the periodic reports described earlier, managers rely on what might be called *special-project* (or *special-needs*) reports, which typically accompany and present the results of specific studies or investigations. Some of the most common types include proposals, progress reviews, and completion reports, business plans, and marketing plans.

Proposals   A proposal is a unique type of report: a request for authorization for a study or special initiative. As a managerial tool, it is a persuasive and informative message that a writer creates for two reasons: to identify plans for solving a problem (or capturing a new opportunity) and to elicit consequent authorization from the decision-making audience.

> *Example:* Shortly before the turn of this century, many *information technology consultants* presented to prospective clients formal proposals in which they articulated their plans for studying the Y2K readiness for all internal systems that depend on computing.

Progress reviews   A progress review brings readers up to date on the status of some ongoing activity, such as a specific study or even regular ongoing operations. Readers use progress reports for a variety of reasons: To keep apprised of the status of the activity, to determine whether it seems to be meeting its prescribed goals, and to decide whether to modify the activity by, for example, devoting more (or fewer) resources to it or eliminating it.

Completion reports   Completion reports provide solutions to problems via specific findings, conclusions, and sometimes recommendations. Completion reports are prepared at the end of a study or investigation.

> *Example:* An *outside consulting team* might be asked to help a manufacturing client determine how to capture higher profits from a particular product line. After the team analyzes the problem and then collects and analyzes appropriate data, they might write a completion report to present to the client with the results of their analysis.

Example: An *in-house team* might conduct a study to determine what the company might do to increase the number of female partners. The study might yield a series of recommendations for the firm to implement. At the end of the study, these recommendations, along with corresponding supporting data, might be presented to the executive board in a report. A report like this would likely be designed to inform and persuade: by documenting what was done, learned, concluded, and recommended.

Business plans   Business plans help prospective investors, company executives, and managers to make informed decisions.

Example: Prospective investors (and bank loan officers) would consult a business plan before investing in a new company. They would use the plan to determine risk, likelihood of success, and likely return on investment.

Example: Company executives might request a business plan from each division, so that they might determine which divisions to grow, shrink, or even divest.

Example: Managers might use a business plan to guide their strategic and tactical planning: to determine whether all activities and resources—financial, human, and technological—are effectively aligned to meet the revenue targets for the department or division.

Marketing plans   Marketing plans help executives, managers, and marketing staff members determine and implement marketing initiatives.

Example: The *executive board* of a health services provider that specializes in cardiac care might read a marketing plan to decide on marketing activities for its international services division: how much to spend, what target market customers to pursue, what specific activities to engage in, and over what time period.

Example: The *marketing staff* might use the report to guide their specific activities once the executive board has decided on broad marketing activities.

III. WHAT VIRTUES EFFECTIVE REPORTS SHARE

Despite the many ways that individual reports may differ, they share one general quality: namely, a report is effective only if it gets read, understood, and used by its target audiences. Effective reports must, in the broadest sense, deliver value to their readers. What, then, does it take for reports to achieve this set of goals? Top-quality reports demonstrate three chief virtues: content value, skim value, and clarity.

By applying these chief virtues to all your reports, you will enhance the likelihood that your target audiences will read your reports, fully understand and accept the key information you are conveying, and act appropriately.

1. Content value

Every report that you create must deliver content value to your key readers. That is, once your audiences have finished reading your report, they must be somehow better off than they were before. Since you will most often be communicating with readers who know less than you do about your specific subject, you must choose content—topics, points, and details—likely to be relevant, useful, and significant to them.

This concept—delivering content value—is necessarily abstract and subjective. No specific formula can enable you to determine with absolute certainty what your readers will likely find to be of value. Who, or what, determines value in a report? For reports, the readers determine value—just as, in companies that produce tangible goods or services, the consumer determines value. Hence, the more you know about your readers, the better you can determine what they are likely to find valuable.

As you prepare to deliver value to your readers in each report, then, you should shape your message so that you meet—and, where possible, exceed—your readers' expectations. You best ensure that you meet and exceed expectations by determining and then testing content value.

Determining content value   To determine what information will provide your readers with the greatest content value, you need to decide what and how much to address. That is, you should make informed choices concerning the scope of your coverage, the quality of your insights, and the depth of your coverage.

- *Scope of topics:* An effective report covers breadth sufficient to meet your readers' needs and accomplish your communication goals. You need to choose: How many topics? Which ones? And why these, specifically?

  Example: A *business plan* is likely to address some variation of the following topics: the company's specific mission; the company's product or service; the competition and market niche; the management team; the organization structure; and the key financial information, including funding request and payback strategy.

- *Quality of insights:* An effective report provides information likely to be of insight or news to your audience. What in your message is likely to be new(s) to your readers? What can they learn from your report that is otherwise unavailable or inaccessible from other sources?

  Example: An *association* devoted to helping graphic design firms improve their businesses might commission a study of the quality of the educational programming that the association makes available to its membership at its semiannual international conventions. The report that results from that study would likely deliver value if it addresses information that will help those responsible for educational programming make informed decisions concerning, for instance, specific workshop topics and outcomes; length, sequence, and frequency of sessions; selection of speakers and workshop facilitators; and so forth.

- *Depth of discussion:* An effective report supports all key assertions with appropriate depth: illustrations, explanations, elaborations, and concrete details. You can help your readers by making explicit what exactly you mean by your assertions; why your readers should accept your assertions; and what actions, if any, you recommend to your readers.

  Example: After reviewing the financial performance of the leading pharmaceutical companies, an investment counselor might conclude that the stock offerings from a particular company are particularly unattractive. Should that counselor report her conclusion to her clients, she would need to be very specific. First, what is the basis for her conclusion?

Second, what specific action is she recommending: that clients divest themselves of that company's holdings—or that they merely refrain from purchasing more from that company?

Testing content value   If your report meets the test of content value, the readers should find it relatively easy to identify the answers to the following questions:

- *Purposes:* What are the chief purposes of the report?
- *Governing question:* The governing question is the question to which your audience seeks an answer. So ask, what specific governing question does the report address?
- *Governing thought:* The governing thought answers the question "What's new?" So ask, what meaningful answer(s) to the governing question does the report provide?
- *Subtopics:* What main subtopics (and corresponding subquestions) does the report address?
- *Main points:* What chief assertions does the report convey concerning each subtopic (or subquestion)?
- *Evidence:* What specific evidence does the report provide to support, illustrate, and elaborate upon each main assertion?

2. Skim value

In addition to delivering content value, effective reports should secure high skim value. *Skim value* means report design that makes it easy for your readers to skim the report and process your ideas. The more difficult it is for your readers to process your ideas, the less likely they will be to read your report and understand from it the key ideas that you wish to convey. (See pages 65–71 for more details on skim value.)

By designing a report high in skim value, you enable your readers to understand your purposes and governing question; to find your key topics, key points, and supporting data; and to skim or skip parts of your report as they see fit. You can achieve high skim value in your reports by making your message conclusion oriented, by choosing effective document-design tools, and by using a clear and logical structure.

Conclusion orientation   A conclusion-oriented message makes your conclusions for each key topic easy for your audiences to find and understand. To make your messages conclusion oriented, you need to surface your key ideas in two sets of places: (1) in the opening of your message, and (2) at the beginning of each segment and paragraph throughout the middle of your report.

- *Surfacing your highest-level conclusion(s) in your opening:* If your message has a highest-level conclusion and/or recommendations, you help your readers by stating that conclusion and/or recommendations up front.

- *Surfacing your next-level conclusions throughout your report:* Throughout your report discussion, you can help your readers find and understand your key ideas if you present your points first and then follow with your elaboration. Once you surface your main point up front in each paragraph, use the rest of the paragraph to elaborate as appropriate: provide explanation, detail, examples, and other supporting data.

To help you surface your highest-level conclusion, remind yourself about the governing thought that answers your governing question. That thought yields your highest-level conclusion.

Example: If a client asks you to assess four mutual funds as investment alternatives, you need not provide your detailed analysis of each fund *before* identifying which you recommend. Instead, provide your highest-level conclusion up front, and then go on, as necessary, to explain your reasoning.

Remember, however, that different governing questions will yield correspondingly different governing thoughts and, hence, different highest-level conclusions.

Example: Continuing with the example above, the following three governing questions will yield three different conclusions:

- Should we continue to invest in the four funds we invested in last year?
- Which of the four will provide the best returns in the next 18 months?
- Should we broaden our portfolio?

Document design   By applying document-design tools and principles to enhance your report's skim value, you can enhance the likelihood that your target audience will read your report, understand your key ideas, and act appropriately. Consider the following features that many well-designed reports use (and see pages 65–71 for more details on document design).

- *Visual appeal:* Your reports should be inviting, rather than a struggle or burden to read. Don't overload the page or any part of it. (1) Use manageable-sized paragraphs: rarely longer than 12 lines. (2) Use modest-length sentences: varied in length but rarely longer than three lines. (3) Use easily readable fonts: serif fonts (for long prose passages) rarely smaller than 11 points. (4) Use standard page margins: roughly an inch at the left and right margins, and 1½ inches at the top and bottom of the · page.

- *Segment headings:* Use carefully labeled and formatted segment headings to guide your readers to the main topics and subtopics you address.

- *Section previews:* Provide a prose passage to introduce and synthesize the key ideas from an ensuing discussion.

- *Visuals:* Use visuals—tables, graphs, charts, and diagrams, as appropriate—to illustrate relationships among topics and data sets.

- *Lists:* Use lists to make it easy for your readers to find, understand, and retrieve a series of items.

- *Attachments:* Use appendices to enable readers to distinguish your primary discussion from information that might be secondary in importance or so detailed that it might prove unduly interruptive if it were placed within the main discussion.

Clear and logical structure   Most effective writers differentiate among a report's three main structural components: the opening, middle, and closing.

- *Opening:* The opening should orient your readers to the detailed discussion that follows in the middle of the message. Depending on how familiar your readers are with the report subject, you may meet your readers' opening needs by addressing four features: the circumstances that prompted you to write, your purpose for writing, your main point, and a preview of the main topics you will address in the ensuing discussion.

- *Middle:* The middle, or body, is where writers develop their discussion of key topics. The challenge in the middle is to shape the message— that is, select and sequence the topics—so that the readers can find each topic and main point; easily understand the logical relationship between topics; and differentiate the main topics and main points from subtopics, subpoints, and supporting detail and elaboration.
- *Closing:* The closing should provide the readers with a sense of closure— a sense of completion. Rather than merely stopping when you are through discussing the key topics in the middle of your message, you can secure closure in a variety of ways. Many consulting presentations, for instance, close by addressing next steps: who does what next? An alternative clos- ing technique would be to address general courtesies: thanking and/or offering further assistance to your audience. Finally, you may want to secure emphasis: by restating the importance of your key ideas.

3. Clarity

Being clear is a fundamental virtue of effective communication. To be clear, you need to do more than merely say what you mean. You need to choose your phrasing carefully, so that you make it easy for your audience to process your message: to understand your purpose, your key points, and all corresponding ideas that support, illustrate, and elaborate upon those key points. By phrasing your ideas with maxi- mum clarity, you secure minimum confusion for your readers.

In a report that demonstrates maximum clarity, every word must tell: that is, every word must convey meaning to the readers. If your reader has to read any phrase, sentence, paragraph, section—or the entire message—more than once just to understand what you are try- ing to convey, then chances are you are not being clear enough. For a clear message should require that the audience read it only once in order to comprehend it. The reader may elect to re-read the message in order to better remember the key points and topics or to get a better sense of the relative weight of the key points. But he or she shouldn't need to do so just to understand what you mean.

You can secure a clear and transparent style for your reports by following the guidelines described on pages 60–64.

WHAT REPORTS WILL YOU PREPARE AT WORK?

The next time you accept a new position—whether you receive a promotion within your department, join a new department, or move to a new company—you can enhance your likelihood of success by finding out about the reports you will be expected to produce. Contact your predecessors, supervisor, and peers to request report samples and discover answers to these questions.

- What types of reports are produced in the position, department, and company?

- Who produces them? At what level are they produced? Within departments? Individual business units? Corporate headquarters?

- What are the purposes for each report?

- Who are the target audiences for each report?

- How are the reports used? To what ends? To help whom make what decisions?

- What kinds of information do these reports contain? Mere data? Conclusions? Recommendations?

- What specific reports will you be expected to produce in your position? Why? When? How often? For whom?

- What specific reports would you be expected to produce in your next position should you soon be promoted?

To prepare reports that will help you and your colleagues accomplish your professional goals—as well as enable you to create, maintain, and/or enhance your credibility—you will need to manage your report-writing process. As the following chapter explains in detail, the most successful report writers manage their process by making sound choices as they plan, shape, and deliver their reports. More specifically, they waste little time as they collect, select, synthesize, and sequence information: namely, the data, conclusions, and perhaps even recommendations that they present in their reports.

CHAPTER 2 OUTLINE

I. THE CONTEXTUAL TASK: PLANNING
   1. Communication strategy
   2. Research strategy

II. THE TECHNICAL TASK:
    RESEARCHING AND ANALYZING
    1. Gather the data
    2. Interpret the data
    3. Identify the solution

III. THE COMPOSING TASK: COMMUNICATING
     1. Structure
     2. Write
     3. Deliver

CHAPTER 2

How to Manage the Report-Writing Process

Your success as a report writer depends on more than just your ability to write. It also depends, in large part, on your ability to develop a system to plan and execute the entire project that culminates in a report—what we call the *report-writing process*. You should approach your reports systematically—that is, in a series of stages, as illustrated below—by attending to the following challenges: (1) the contextual task (planning your communication strategy and research strategy), (2) the technical task (researching and analyzing findings), and (3) the composing task (communicating).

MANAGING THE REPORT-WRITING PROCESS		
Contextual Task: Planning ➡	**Technical Task:** Researching and Analyzing ➡	**Composing Task:** Communicating

1. Communication strategy
 	
2. Research strategy
	1. Gather data
	  • Locating data
	  • Securing easy
	    retrieval
	
	2. Interpret data
	
	3. Identify solution
	  • Recommendations
	  • Key conclusions
		1. Structure
		
		2. Write
		
		3. Deliver

Although the report-writing process may appear to be lockstep, remember that it is, in fact, recursive. That is, you may occasionally jump ahead a few stages and/or return to earlier stages in the process as you continually reassess your progress. If you develop a system for problem solving when you create and shape reports, you will:

- *Uncover the key data* that you will communicate in your report. Only by managing your process well can you be sure that you have identified what specific information to gather, analyze, and present in your report.

- *Enhance your versatility* because you will be able to adapt your problem-solving skills to virtually any reporting challenge or situation: routine or unique; large or small; focused exclusively on data or, more broadly, on data and analysis.

- *Minimize the time* you spend unproductively and enhance the quality of your report outcome. If you manage your projects well, you are likely to spend less time on your reports—and emerge with better quality solutions—in comparison to those who do not manage their projects well.

- *Improve your satisfaction* during the entire problem-solving process. You are more likely to maintain your motivation, decrease or forestall any frustration, and see how each step in the process helps contribute meaningfully toward your report outcome. And if you manage your project well when you collaborate on a report, you will likely help your teammates capture the same benefits.

To capture these benefits throughout every stage of the report-writing process, keep focused on your central goal: to solve the problem you set out to address. Always look ahead toward finding and presenting to your readers the best solution—the best answer to your governing question.

I. CONTEXTUAL TASK: PLANNING

Your contextual task calls for you to plan the report-writing process by conducting analysis so that you may develop a communication strategy and a research strategy. After you have engaged in this analysis, you should have a clear understanding of who wants to know the answers to what question—and why. Further, you should understand what specific information—and from which specific sources—will help you to achieve your project goals.

Effective report writers will typically spend a great deal of time at this stage: extra planning time spent up front diminishes the likelihood that you will misspend time later. Put differently, for each hour you devote to careful planning, you are likely to save exponential multiples later on, during the subsequent research, analysis, and communication stages.

MANAGING THE REPORT-WRITING PROCESS		
Contextual Task: Planning ➤	**Technical Task: Researching and Analyzing** ➤	**Composing Task: Communicating**

1. Communication strategy
 	
2. Research strategy
	1. Gather data
	  • Locating data
	  • Securing easy retrieval
	
	2. Interpret data
	
	3. Identify solution
	  • Recommendations
	  • Key conclusions
		1. Structure
		
		2. Write
		
		3. Deliver

1. Communication strategy

Planning your communication strategy calls for you to identify your project goal, your readers and their needs, the project deliverables, and your resources. We will use the following example to illustrate each of these communication strategy features.

> *Communication strategy example:* The leaders of an international consumer-products company might recognize that their executive ranks are virtually exclusively male—and that women seem to be leaving the company at an alarming rate. They might, then, set up an internal task force to investigate and identify solutions.

Project goals   Your first step should be to determine your project goals, because your project goals drive all the other choices you make as you manage your problem-solving process. To determine your project goals, consider the following questions:

- What specifically are you trying to accomplish in your report?
- What outcomes do you expect after your project is complete?

> *The goals:* The project goals might be to determine whether the company is, in fact, unfriendly to women employees, and to identify methods for improving the situation. The outcome might be a set of recommendations for the readers to consider, decide on, and implement.

Readers   Your next step should entail identifying your key readers and determining their needs. Consider the following questions:

- Who will read your report and use the information it contains?
- How will they use the information in your report? What specifically will they want to learn? What specific decisions, if any, will they make based on the data, conclusions, and recommendations your report contains?
- What specifically should you address in your report so that you can be confident that you enable your readers to use your report as they see fit?
- What specifically might you do in your report to meet—and, where possible, exceed—your readers' expectations?

> *The readers:* The task force might identify key readers as those who would decide on any changes and those who might be charged with exe-

cuting any changes. These might include senior-level company executives responsible for operations, human resources, corporate communications, as well as vice-presidents of the company divisions.

Project deliverables   Finally, you should identify the project deliverables. That is, you should plan the specific points at which you will communicate meaningfully with your readers throughout your problem-solving process. Consider the following:

- When and how often during the problem-solving process will you communicate with your key readers? (Might you, for instance, use progress reviews to forestall resistance to your conclusions and recommendations? Might you follow up shortly after you have presented your final deliverable?) What channels might you use for these communication opportunities?
- What will your final deliverable look like? How long will it likely be? To what degree will it combine prose text, numerical data, and charts and graphs?

The deliverables: Depending on the duration of the study, the task force might plan a series of progress reviews, to inform the readers of interim findings, as well as a completion report that might present specific recommendations, conclusions, and findings.

Resources   In addition to analyzing your project goals, readers, and deliverables as part of your communication strategy, you should consider other resources that you might need to take advantage of.

- Will you work as part of a team to complete your project? If so, who will be responsible for what specific activities: gathering unique data, analyzing sets of findings, drafting parts—or the whole—of the report?
- Will you need additional assistance from researchers, statisticians, graphic-design specialists? Will you use an editor or colleague to review any of your drafts?

The resources: The task force might engage the services of support staff to conduct research, analyze statistical findings, and create charts and graphs that present historical comparisons.

2. Research strategy

Planning your research strategy calls for you to identify your governing question, the subtopics and subquestions you will need to address, and the research sources and methods you will use to gather data. The example that follows continues the illustration begun earlier and depicts the complementary relationship among all three research strategy features.

Governing question   Before you begin conducting any research, you need to identify your governing question. That is, given the goals and reader needs you identified as part of your communication strategy, what specific question are you trying to answer for your audience? As the illustration below indicates, by phrasing your governing question carefully, you will make it easier to identify appropriate research sources and methods, find the data you need, and shape the data into a report that meets the needs of your key readers.

> *The governing question:* The members of the task force might identify the following governing question for their study: how to attract, retain, grow, and promote women into top management positions? A governing question phrased more narrowly, such as why women are leaving, would yield a report more limited in scope and, hence, be inadequate to address the project goals and the expectations of the key readers.

Subtopics and subquestions   Once you have articulated your governing question, you should continue planning your research by "unpacking" the governing question and identifying an exhaustive list of component parts: subtopics and subquestions. Consider the following:

- What specific subtopics should you explore to help you answer the governing question?
- What specific questions might you address concerning each subtopic?
- What specific data will likely be of value to you and your readers?

> *The subtopics and subquestions:* Task-force members might identify a host of subtopics and questions, of which the following are just a few. (1) *The actual situation:* Are women leaving the firm at a higher rate than men? Are they leaving from comparable positions? (2) *Historical comparison:* What trends are apparent over the past

five years? How do these recent trends compare to those evident from an earlier five-year period? (3) *Causes or sources of workplace satisfaction and dissatisfaction:* What features attract women to the company? What features keep them? What factors cause them to leave? (4) *Situations at comparable companies:* How successful are comparable companies? Which companies are most successful? Least? Based on what factors?

Research methods and sources   If you have thoughtfully identified the specific subtopics and corresponding subquestions that you need to address, you should find it relatively easy to identify the specific research you should engage in to gather the data you need. Consider the following:

- What specific sources would be able to provide you with the data you seek to answer each key sub-question? Company files? On-line databases? Individuals working within your company or for other firms? Other sources?
- What specific methods might you use to gather the specific data you seek? Interviews? Surveys? Focus groups?

The research sources and methods: The task-force members might engage in a variety of research approaches, of which the following are just a few. (1) Use company files to identify a range of demographic information concerning women employed by the company during a particular period, such as the most recent five years. (2) Identify specific women who have departed—and remained—as targets for surveys, focus groups, and interviews. (3) Consult published sources and subject-area specialists, as well as associations that address the unique needs and interests of professional women.

II. TECHNICAL TASK:
RESEARCHING AND ANALYZING

The *technical task* calls for you to solve whatever problem you set out to address. In other words, you need to conduct the necessary research—gather the data and analyze it appropriately—so that you can identify solutions: the answer to the governing question that you have set out to address in your project.

MANAGING THE REPORT-WRITING PROCESS		
Contextual Task: Planning ➡	**Technical Task: Researching and Analyzing** ➡	**Composing Task: Communicating**
1. Communication strategy 2. Research strategy	1. Gather data • Locating data • Securing easy retrieval 2. Interpret data 3. Identify solution • Recommendations • Key conclusions	1. Structure 2. Write 3. Deliver

I. Gather the data

As you gather the data that you will use as a basis for your report, you need to conduct research carefully. If you have planned your research strategy well, you now need to execute that strategy thoughtfully: (1) by systematically locating all your primary and secondary data, and (2) by securing easy retrieval for all your data. Consider the following.

Locating your data   Depending on your unique project needs, you will typically locate and collect your data from primary and secondary sources.

- *Primary data* refers to the information you might gather that has not been published. These data sources include individuals whom you might interview, focus groups you might facilitate, company files or databases you might consult, surveys you might conduct, and statistical or other types of information that you generate yourself to help you answer your research subquestions. Because you are responsible for the accuracy and reliability of primary data, you should be especially careful as you record it and use it: Your credibility is on the line.

- *Secondary data* refers to the information you might gather from published sources. These data sources include articles published in the popular, business, or other specialized press; books; information taken from the World Wide Web; and more. What characterizes secondary data is that someone has already collected the information. Hence, if you use secondary information, you should be sure to select it from only credible sources and, in turn, acknowledge the specific source when you use the information.

Securing easy retrieval   You should approach your data-collection process systematically. More specifically, you should consider how you will record and organize all of your data findings, so that you can retrieve them as you accomplish two goals. (1) As you seek to answer each specific research subquestion, you will need to retrieve the appropriate specific data. (2) Once you are ready to compose your report, you will need to be able to find the specific data findings appropriate for each section, so that you can surface, support, and illustrate your assertions. Consider the following techniques that might help you achieve these goals:

- *Read and take notes from written and statistical source material:* Use an effective and systematic approach—via note cards, note sheets, or computer database systems, such as Excel, Lotus 1-2-3, Access, or others. These computer programs allow you to compile, store, and retrieve data in various formats for analysis. On each note card, note sheet, or database system, identify your data source accurately.

- *Record findings from any interviews or focus groups:* Distinguish between direct quotations and paraphrases.

- *Capture your own comments, in addition to the data findings from sources:* Use your own comments to interpret or otherwise elaborate on the source information, showing how that information is significant. By capturing your own interpretive comments as you record source data, you enhance the likelihood that you will later remember what you found especially important about the specific data you have collected.

- *Organize your data by subtopic, rather than by source:* By organizing your data by subtopic—according to the subtopics and subquestions that you identified as you planned your research strategy—you should simplify the later steps when you interpret your data, identify solutions, and compose your report.

2. Interpret the data

As you interpret the data you have collected, you analyze your research findings so that you can answer your specific subquestions. If you have planned your research strategy well, gathered your data effectively, and organized your data by topics and subtopics, you should find that these steps directly lead you to the answers to your governing question. For your data analysis, try using an inquiry-based approach:

- Group your data according to subtopics appropriate to your project.

- Identify the central question you are trying to answer for each subtopic.

- For each specific subquestion you have identified, tease out the answer from the data. Elicit meaning—one or more generalizations, as appropriate—from each data grouping.

- Assemble your specific data in support of each assertion. If your readers were to ask you to provide the evidence that supports each assertion of yours, what specific evidence would you provide?

3. Identify the solution.

The final step in your technical task calls for you to determine the answer to the governing question that has driven your entire project. As you seek to answer your governing question, you need to determine what you want your readers to know and, as appropriate, what you want the readers to do. Consider the following alternatives:

- *Uninterpreted data:* If, based on your analysis of your contextual task, you have determined that your readers seek data without interpretation, simply group your data according to the subtopics you have identified.

- *Conclusions:* If, instead, you have determined that your readers would expect you to draw conclusions from the data you have collected, group your data by subtopic and use the data to determine the answers to each subquestion.

- *Single assertion:* Reduce each conclusion to a single assertion: if you were limited to one sentence to summarize what you have learned from each data grouping, what would that sentence be?

- *Recommendation(s):* If, based on your analysis of your contextual task, you have determined that your readers seek recommendations to accompany your conclusions and data, generalize further from your conclusions and data. That is, given the conclusions you have identified, what specifically would you recommend that your readers do? What specific action steps should they consider?

III. COMPOSING TASK: COMMUNICATING

After you have completed your technical task—that is, discovered the solution to your problem—you should attend to your composing task: creating an effective report that delivers the news to your readers. Focus on shaping your report so that you can be confident that your audiences will read it and understand, accept, and act on the key ideas it conveys. Review the communication strategy that you identified earlier (see pages 26–27) and then manage your composing task by structuring, writing, and delivering your report.

MANAGING THE REPORT-WRITING PROCESS		
Contextual Task: Planning ➡	**Technical Task: Researching and Analyzing** ➡	**Composing Task: Communicating**

1. Communication strategy
 	
2. Research strategy
	1. Gather data
	  • Locating data
	  • Securing easy retrieval
	
	2. Interpret data
	
	3. Identify solution
	  • Recommendations
	  • Key conclusions
		1. Structure
		
		2. Write
		
		3. Deliver

I. Structure

The first step in the composing process is to identify a tentative structure for your report. What specific topics—and in what sequence—will you address?

Some report writers go wrong at this stage. For instance, those who do not understand the fundamental differences between the technical task and the communication task sometimes structure their messages by retracing their discovery process: merely recounting the process by which they arrived at the solution. As you prepare a report, though, you need to liberate yourself from the path that led to your solution.

Instead of structuring your message according to your discovery process, devise a message that focuses on your solutions: the news. That is, you should choose a structure that will enable you to focus on the key information likely to be of interest to the report readers. Depending on the individual project challenge, that information is likely to be recommendations, conclusions, and/or key findings. Consider the following guidelines as you shape the component parts of the report body: a distinct opening, middle, and closing for your report.

Opening Determine what preliminary information your readers need. What information should you provide up front to guide your readers to the detailed information that follows?

Middle Generate a tentative outline for the segments in the middle of your report. Given your tentative answer to your governing question, determine how best to state, shape, and support the answer. You should create an audience-centered message by structuring your topics according to the needs of the readers. That is, you should not structure your report by sequencing your topics in the order you thought of them or in the order in which you discovered them. Instead, you should structure your report by sequencing your topics so that your readers will understand, accept, and act on your key ideas.

To determine the sequence of topics most suitable for your readers, analyze your readers to determine how much or little they already know about your overall report project and how likely they will be to accept the data (and, as appropriate, the conclusions and recommendations) you present in your report. Adapt to their existing knowledge and consequent needs by considering the following questions:

- What specific topics should your report address? In what groupings?
- What questions would your readers be likely to raise concerning those topics?
- Which questions or topics would your readers need for you to address first? Second? Why in this sequence?
- What questions or topics might you cover as supplementary information (i.e., attachments)?

Closing   Determine how to close your report. Will you provide a recap of your key points? Will you offer further assistance? Will you identify next steps in the problem-solving process: who does what next?

2. Write

After you have identified a tentative structure for your report, you should begin writing—generating the prose that will serve as the foundation of your report. For even the most skilled writers, however, the first draft of a document is rarely a message they can be proud of. Instead, most first drafts resemble a "data dump": rough; messy; filled with false starts, random ideas, misspellings, typographical errors; and the like. But a very rough first draft is okay. For when top-performing writers compose especially important, lengthy, complex, or challenging messages, they often try to accomplish different objectives at each drafting stage: in their first draft and in their revised drafts.

First draft   The first draft of your report need not be perfect; it will never be seen by your key readers. Its function is simply to help you arrive at a sound final draft.

An early draft may lack a perfect structure, appropriate support for all assertions, clear and precise phrasing, and error-free mechanics. When you compose your earliest draft, you need not perfect your words, sentences, or paragraphs, grammar, spelling, or typing. Rather, you should simply try to get your wealth of ideas on paper: record your ideas with some semblance of organization. Strengthening, tightening, and polishing will come as you revise.

- Begin composing the opening of your message, and then draft the middle of the report one segment at a time, based on your outline. The key, simply, is to break the writing into manageable-sized pieces—one segment at a time—and capture your ideas on paper. Even modest progress is progress.
- You need not draft your segments in the sequence that they will appear in your report. If you encounter writer's block as you approach any segment, consider switching to a different segment.
- Continue composing until you generate a complete draft.

Revised drafts   Once you have a complete draft, you should review it and prepare to revise it. Modify it as appropriate. (1) Consider how you might improve the report's substantive features (i.e., content, structure, and conclusion orientation). (2) Consider how you might improve the report's surface features (i.e., skim value, sentence-level style, and correctness).

As you review the substantive features of your first draft, you should focus on the structure and content of your report: what you might add to, delete from, or rearrange within your prose message.

- *Do you need to modify your content?* Does your report present appropriate evidence to support and illustrate your chief conclusions and recommendations? Does your report have any significant content gaps? Does it address unnecessary topics or provide unnecessary details and examples?
- *Do you need to modify your structure?* Do segments overlap? Is the sequence of topics appropriate for your readers? Do you assemble similar sets of topics into larger groupings?
- *Do you need to improve your conclusion orientation within any segments and paragraphs?* Do you surface a governing thought in each segment and paragraph? Is each unit coherent? Do you guide your readers through your discussion in each unit?

After you modify the substantive features of your first draft, you should focus on surface features so that you phrase all your ideas clearly and concisely, secure high skim value, and ensure that your report is error free.

- *Revise for skim value:* Do you use segment headings, lists, topic sentences, and manageable-sized paragraphs throughout your report? Do you use format features consistently? Can your readers distill your key topics and points by skim-reading the message?

- *Revise for sentence-level style:* Does each sentence convey an idea clearly and concisely?

- *Revise for correctness:* Is the message free from errors? After you have revised all other features, proofread a printed copy of your report, and correct any errors involving grammar, mechanics, and carelessness.

3. Deliver

After you have revised your report, you need to deliver it. You or your support staff need to attend to specific tasks: printing, copying, collating, binding, and distributing the report final draft to your key readers. Be sure to attend to these tasks with the same degree of care with which you approached the rest of your project: follow up as necessary, for careless errors at this final stage might undermine much of the good work you have completed at the earlier stages.

———————

Each of these three tasks—your contextual task, your technical task, and your composing task—poses unique challenges that vary in complexity, depending on the individual project. Sometimes, the technical task is the most challenging. Other times, the communication task proves daunting, especially when your final deliverable is a lengthy report, based on which your readers may make decisions that affect the lives of countless employees and the finances of countless others. Invariably, though, unless you have carefully planned your project and executed your research, the quality of your solution may be undermined. However, if you thoughtfully attend to these three tasks, you will likely have the data you need—as well as appropriate conclusions and recommendations—that will enable you to make informed choices as you shape your reports.

The following chapter provides you with more specific report guidelines, so that you can make informed choices as you shape the front-end materials, the report body, and the back-end materials.

CHAPTER 3 OUTLINE

  I. FRONT-END MATERIALS
    1. Write transmittal document
    2. Summarize your report for the executive reader
    3. Design your title page and table of contents

  II. BODY OF THE REPORT
    1. Introduce the project and governing questions
    2. Answer the governing questions
    3. Develop your rationale and supporting ideas
    4. Close the report

  III. BACK-END MATERIALS
    1. Use appendices to improve usability
    2. Document sources in your bibliography

CHAPTER 3

What Key Elements to Include in a Report

Chapter 2 outlined an effective writing process for business reports. Begin with the contextual task of exploring your communication strategy and developing your research strategy; move to a technical task of gathering data and identifying solutions; and finish with a communication task focused on structuring, writing, and delivering your report. All this talk of process leads to one very important question: Now that we know *how* to go about writing a report, *what* exactly do we write? The answer to that question depends on which component of the report you are writing. You should place different materials at the front of the report than you do within the body and at the back.

This chapter, which covers front-end materials, report body, and back-end materials, should help you understand how to craft specific pieces of information into your report and implement your communication strategy.

I. FRONT-END MATERIALS

Front-end materials help orient your readers to the report. Orienting your readers can mean several things. First, you may want to build goodwill with your audience through a gracious letter of transmittal. You also usually need to provide essential findings and recommendations in your executive summary. Finally, be sure to include essential information on the title page, and consider pointing your readers to specific sections with your table of contents.

1. Write a transmittal document

Report writing is more than just an analytical task. It requires interpersonal skills as well as analytical ones. The transmittal letter or memo presents you, the report writer, with your only real opportunity to write directly to the reader. You should feel free to write in the first or second person using personal pronouns such as *we* or *you*. When written well, a transmittal letter or memo will set a favorable tone and invite the reader to see the report as one part of a larger problem-solving or decision-making context. (See page 75 for an example of a transmittal document.)

Here are three issues to consider when you write a transmittal document.

Choosing between letter and memo   You should write a memo if you are transmitting your report internally and a letter if you are transmitting your report externally to a client. In large, multinational firms where the distinction between internal and external to the company can sometimes become blurred, look to existing organizational standards for guidance.

Summarizing key ideas in the report   Your strategy depends on whether you are writing an executive summary (discussed in the following section). If you are not writing a separate executive summary, then it would be appropriate to present key conclusions and recommendations in your transmittal document. Otherwise, keep your transmittal document short and focused on the report's purpose and building goodwill.

Establishing a cordial tone   Use a cordial tone that is not excessive. You want the reader to be reminded of the report's business purpose, and you want those who played key roles to feel appreciated. If a client hired you to create a report, this is an ideal opportunity to express your appreciation. As a rule of thumb, keep your tone pleasant and your gratitude sincere and concise. Long-winded pleasantries can become tiring and look amateurish.

2. Summarize your report for the executive reader

The executive summary may be the single most important element of a business report. The executive summary opens a window into the body of the report and allows the reader to quickly see how well you have managed your message. The executive summary is written for the business professionals engaged in decision-making and policy-setting activities: the typical business executives found in middle and upper management. (See page 77 for a sample executive summary.)

The executive summary becomes a critical element in the problem-solving process because many business executives never read the entire report. Instead, they may read only the executive summary, listen to a report presentation, and ask key questions. If time is available or if the decision makers are especially interested in the project, they may read individual sections of the report. It would be a mistake, however, to assume that all parties involved will take the time to read the entire report.

The executive summary is critical, therefore, because it is the one element of your report you can expect everyone to read. You must take special care to design an effective message that speaks *directly and concisely* to the governing project questions. Write your executive summary last. It will be much easier to capture the essence of your report if you first finish processing and organizing ideas in the report.

How long should the executive summary be?   The shorter the executive summary, the better—so long as it fulfills its function as a summary of the report that follows. A brief business report may have only a one-page or shorter executive summary. Longer business reports may go to a two-page summary. No matter how long your report is, you should rarely write an executive summary longer than two or three pages. Anything longer might cease to be a summary. The length of your executive summary should be proportional to the length of your report, which means that summaries longer than a few pages will be rare.

What to include in the executive summary?   First and foremost, you need to present the key conclusions and recommendations from your report. If you are writing a report to help a portfolio manager at a financial institution reduce exposure to risk, then recognize your audience's decision-making responsibilities and prioritize your recommendations for reducing risk (the points at which decisions need to be made). You may want to include very select pieces of supporting data if you have uncovered information that is particularly important. As a rule, however, you don't need to include substantial quantities of supporting data in your executive summary. Instead, you should keep the summary short, focus on answers to the governing questions, and put most of the supporting information in the body of your report.

What to say about the project's history or methodology?   Base this decision on the needs of your audience. Are you writing to people who may not have knowledge of your project? If so, a brief project description may be in order. Will knowledge of your research methodology help your audience make a better decision or improve their performance? If not, consider discussing your methodology only in the report or in an appendix.

3. Design your title page and table of contents

Creating an effective title page and table of contents can be a relatively simple part of writing your report. In this age of technology, you can create professional and visually inviting pages with nothing more than a couple of clicks of the mouse. Applying technology along with the following content guidelines should help you complete the essential front-end materials of a business report. (See pages 79 and 81 for examples.)

Include four essential points on the title page   Effective title pages will usually contain the following pieces of information.

- *Report title:* The name of your report will typically be centered on the page and near the top. All capital letters are commonly used to help the report name appear boldly on the page.

- *Presented to:* Who is the audience for your report? Clearly write the name, position, and organization of the person receiving your report. Center this information and place it near the middle of the page.
- *Presented by:* Who wrote the report? Write your name and any essential identifying information such as your title or organization. This information should be centered near the bottom of the page.
- *Date:* On what date are you delivering the report to the recipient? Center the date below the "Presented by" information.

Present essential ideas in the table of contents   While the table of contents (TOC) should be one of the last items you write (even after the executive summary), it should not be written carelessly. An effective TOC will help your reader locate desired information and move directly to that segment of the report. In other words, an effective TOC dramatically improves the usability of your business report.

Many word processing applications will now construct a table of contents for you. With informative headings (discussed on pages 65–67), you can quickly and easily construct an effective TOC simply by clicking a mouse. Using writing software (e.g., Microsoft Word) to create your TOC *requires* that you include technology in your prewriting plans and fully understand how to properly set up and integrate the program's features into your writing practices. Not knowing how to use your software can lead to wasted time and energy in last-minute editing, rewriting, and redesigning of your report.

II. BODY OF THE REPORT

The main body of your business report should be constructed with your audience, and answers to the governing questions, in mind. How will your audience use the document, and what questions are they most interested in or curious about? If your audience is engaged in decision making or problem solving, they are likely to be most interested in your recommendations. In effect, the recommendations identify the points at which decisions need to be made and provide a starting point for thought and discussion.

While reports can take many different shapes and appearances (as explained on pages 9–13), several design elements are commonly found in reports. These elements are the introduction and/or problem statement, answers to the governing questions, support and rationale for answers to governing questions, and closing comments.

1. Introduce the project and governing questions

The reader's need for introductory comments can vary greatly. When your readers are very familiar with the project, your report may need little more than a two- or three-sentence paragraph for opening comments. When your readers' familiarity with your project is limited, your report may require much more of an introduction. An extensive introduction provides information that is necessary for helping the reader follow and comprehend the information that follows. You can quickly and easily orient your readers and improve their ability to comprehend the report body by first explaining *what, why,* and *how.* These three elements of a report opening invite the audience to continue reading and help make the report usable and understandable.

What is this report about?   What is the governing question that prompted this report? What is your purpose in composing this report? You need to be able to articulate, simply and directly, the governing question and main purpose of this report.

Why should the audience be concerned?   Why should the audience make time in their busy day to read this report? The key issue here is common ground. Do you understand the needs and concerns of your audience to the point that you can say, in very simple terms, exactly how this report will benefit them? Your ability to articulate your understanding of your audience's needs can be a powerful tool for building common ground and motivating the audience to read on.

One effective technique for expressing your understanding of audience interests is to discuss benefits instead of features. Features are characteristics of an object, while benefits are what the audience gains by employing a feature.

Feature: This automobile has antilock brakes.

Benefit: You will be able to stop your car on a dime.

Feature: Online banking provides 24-hour access to your accounts.

Benefits: You can access your account anytime, anywhere, and make transfers or changes without waiting.

Understanding the difference between features and benefits will help you build common ground with the audience and to design a report that speaks to the felt needs of the reader.

How is the report organized?   The *how* is essentially a preview placed in the body of your report. Other report elements serving a preview function, such as the executive summary or TOC, come prior to the main report body. By using your introduction to tell your readers where the report is going, you will make it easier for them to understand how all the pieces fit together and to distinguish between essential and nonessential ideas. You can effectively preview your report in two ways:

- A few sentences describing the content of your report.
- A series of informative headings (discussed on pages 65–67) quickly outlining the main topics of your report.

You may want to use both techniques for longer reports. Because longer reports will often present extended and in-depth discussion, readers will find helpful clear signposts that indicate the structure and flow of ideas.

2. Answer the governing questions

One of the most common questions, and sometimes most contentious, is whether you should present your recommendations or findings closer to the front or to the back of the report. In other words, should you organize your report with a direct or indirect pattern of organization?

The answer to this question rests on one important premise—that effective reports are designed with the *readers' needs* in mind. You need to understand exactly what type of work your readers are engaged in and write your report to make that work easier and more effective. You risk designing a poor message when you do not make the audience's needs a primary concern. A document becomes more usable when you design your message to facilitate and enhance the reader's work.

Use a direct pattern to aid decision making   In decision-making, problem-solving, and policy-setting situations, surface your recommendations and conclusions in your executive summary and at the beginning of each paragraph. A report in which the recommendations and conclusions have surfaced is said to have a *direct* pattern of organization. A direct pattern targets the specific needs of decision makers and problem solvers by placing key conclusions and decision-making points where they are most easy for the readers to find them.

As suggested on page 17, a conclusion-oriented message allows main conclusions to surface in your opening and at the beginning of

ANSWER THE GOVERNING QUESTION: DIRECT VS. INDIRECT PATTERN	
Direct Pattern	**Indirect Pattern**
Recommendation 1: Develop an e-commerce strategy	1. Competitive analysis: competition already involved in e-commerce
1. Competition already involved in e-commerce	2. Market potential: $96 million market potential in 2002 and $115 million market potential in 2003
2. $96 million market potential in 2002 and $115 million market potential in 2003	3. Alliances: opportunities to form alliances with existing e-commerce firms
3. Opportunities to form alliances with existing e-commerce firms	(Therefore) ABC Corporation should develop an e-comerce stategy

each section or paragraph. Surfacing conclusions serves to increase the skim value of your report and aid reader comprehension.

Use an indirect pattern to emphasize the validity and reliability of information   Reserve the indirect pattern of organization for process-oriented readers who value knowing the research methodology, research results, and findings *before* reading the recommendations. A report in which the recommendations follow the methodology and findings, a pattern of organization that mirrors the thought processes by which you arrived at your recommendations, is said to have an *indirect* pattern of organization.

You may also want to use an indirect pattern of organization with buried conclusions if you expect your audience to have a *strong* and *negative emotional reaction* to your recommendations. A strong emotional response can inhibit comprehension and provoke an angry or argumentative response from your reader. If you are delivering very difficult news and expect such a reaction, consider presenting your evidence before your conclusions.

3. Develop your rationale and supporting ideas

Once you have determined whether to use a direct or indirect pattern of organization, you must decide how to support or prove the validity of your answers to the governing questions. To phrase this differently, how do you go about supporting the quality of your recommendations?

There are basically three types of support you can provide for your recommendations or conclusions: historical information, methodological information, and hard data. Additionally, you need to ask how much of each data type the audience needs and how you can avoid overloading readers with concrete information.

How to use historical data   Think of historical data as the background or reason for delivering a report. Historical data answers the question, *"Why are you telling me this?"* If you are delivering a series of recommendations to your reader, those recommendations must evolve out of a business problem or concern. What is that concern? What events or observations prompted the concern? Effective report writers can substantiate or support the quality of their recommendations by reminding the reader of the business problem or concern that prompted the report.

Historical information is typically presented in one of two ways: in the report body or in an appendix.

- Some reports may devote one section of the report body to describing the historical background. If understanding the background will help your audience comprehend your recommendations, then place your historical description in the report body.
- Other reports will place the historical information in an appendix. Placing background information in an appendix helps to keep the report brief and avoids forcing readers familiar with the background information to sift through what they already know. Readers who want or need background information can visit the appendix for further reading.

How to use methodological data   What procedures and what rules did you follow when gathering information and generating data? Some readers of your report may be very interested in your data-collection procedure because they want to feel confident that your recommendations are based on reliable and valid information.

As was the case with historical information, methodological information can be presented in either the body or an appendix. Consider your audience, and ask whether or not your methodology is likely to be a critical concern. If it is, consider including methodological data in the report's body. Otherwise, move most or all of your methodological description to the appendix.

In each of the following examples, the essential question being asked is, *"How did you get that information?"* Methodological data provides your readers with answers to this question.

- *When valuing a company,* did you look at the price earnings ratio or did you look at the multiple of cash flow per share? Why did you select one valuation model over the other? What makes your chosen model the appropriate one in this case?
- *When introducing three new salsa products to the marketplace,* did you gather information about customer tastes and preferences? If so, did you conduct focus groups? Did you introduce the products into test markets and gather information about sales and customer reactions?
- *When recommending that a manufacturer introduce new efficiencies into the production process,* did you first diagram the existing process? Have you assessed how capacity, scheduling, inventory, standards, and controls will be impacted by your recommendations? Will employees need to be

trained or will technology need to be updated if your recommendations are implemented? How did you come to these conclusions?

How to use hard data   Hard data can take many forms depending on your approach to gathering information. Typical examples of hard data include financial figures and measures, quotes (e.g., from a focus group), statistical evidence, observations, and examples and illustrations.

Use hard data to answer the question, *"How do you know?"* Hard data allows you to support your point and demonstrate that you have logically and thoughtfully reached your conclusions or recommendations. Most business audiences will not, and should not, accept your recommendations at face value. They will want to know what evidence you have and if your conclusion or recommendation flows logically from that evidence. The burden is on you to prove that you are making good recommendations.

While understanding the types of data available to us is certainly necessary, a mere typology will also be incomplete. We must also consider the sometimes fine line between too little and too much data.

How much data to include   This question can be difficult to answer. Some readers may only look at the executive summary, ask you a few questions, and then move toward a decision. In other instances, an audience may spend hours poring over your data and looking for alternate interpretations or outliers. In this sense, hard data is no different than historical or methodological information. Consider the needs of your audience, and design your report accordingly. You may want to put large bodies of data in the report, or you may want to include only key information in the body and then reference complete bodies of data in your appendix.

How to avoid giving too much information   The one strategy you probably do *not* want to employ is the data dump. The term *data dump* describes large bodies of information that are seemingly "dumped" into the report's body without a clear purpose or coherent flow. Inexperienced report writers have a tendency to create data dumps after spending weeks if not months conducting research and gathering data. Having gathered large quantities of information, inexperienced writers may include so much hard data that the report's narrative flow and coherent logic fades away. You stand an excellent chance of boring—and probably losing—your audience when the report loses its narrative flow and coherent logic.

Here are four hints to help you avoid creating a data dump:

- Focus on the audience's needs rather than trying to demonstrate how much you know or have learned.
- Use a direct pattern of organization that allows main conclusions to surface.
- Avoid organizing your report in a chronological fashion that mirrors the project process.
- Provide only essential supporting data in the report body and place large or complete bodies of information in an appendix.

4. Close the report

The decisions you make when choosing a direct or an indirect structure (pages 48–49) will probably determine whether your closing will be brief or extensive. The shape or design of your close will vary with your decision to organize the report directly or indirectly. Taking the time to think about your closing during the prewriting stages—when you choose between the two different organizational patterns—should help you draft an appropriate ending that serves the reader's needs and reflects positively on your abilities as a business writer.

How to bring a direct pattern of organization to a close   Summarizing the information most desired by the audience is a good technique for closing reports organized according to a direct pattern. Begin by considering the information you are delivering to the reader.

- If your report is designed for an audience that needs data—but does not need or expect to know what to do based on that data—then a discussion of recommendations or implications will probably feel premature.
- If your report is designed for an audience that needs to make decisions based on the data you provide, then a report that does not summarize key decision-making points will probably feel incomplete and result in frustration.

In very general terms, you want your closing to provide sufficient information without overstepping the audience's boundaries or expectations.

If you have organized your report in a direct pattern, you probably will need only a brief closing. The fact that your recommendations were introduced early and discussed fully means that you need not spend much time rehashing these ideas in the closing. A brief ending should suffice.

How to bring an indirect pattern of organization to a close   If you have organized your report indirectly, you may want to use a combination of techniques to help your readers grasp the important ideas and discern how the ideas are interrelated. Specifically, combine the following techniques to help your readers see how your ideas come together in a coherent narrative form.

- *Summarize:* tell your readers, in general terms, what you have been trying to explain. Paint the big picture.
- *Identify:* highlight key findings so the reader knows which points are most important.
- *Articulate:* express your recommendations concisely and directly so that readers understand your suggested course of action.

In comparison to the closing of a direct pattern of organization, the closing of a report that uses an indirect pattern of organization will probably take more space and words since this will be the first place, other than the executive summary, where you have presented your main ideas together in a coherent argument.

III. BACK-END MATERIALS

Back-end materials allow you to include important information without forcing all readers to wade through large bodies of technical, financial, mathematical, historical, research methodological, or procedural information. Back-end materials provide the reader with more complete and detailed information that may be important to some readers but is probably not essential to understanding your main arguments, conclusions, or recommendations.

For example, the body of your report may recommend weight limits for temporary bridges being constructed in a storm-torn country. The complete calculations, however, might be found in an appendix. Readers wanting to "see your math" can quickly refer to the appendix, while those interested in implementing your recommendations may have only a passing interest in the calculations. The implementers in your audience may simply want to read the report without getting bogged down in calculations.

There are two key components of back-end materials: the appendices and bibliography.

1. Use appendices to improve usability

Appendices are intended to supplement or expand upon materials presented in the body of your report. Typically, an appendix will include information that is so detailed or lengthy that, if it were placed in the body of the report, it would diminish your ability to simply and clearly speak to the governing questions of your report. Additionally, appendices should include information that is secondary to the reader's interest but still relevant.

Why use appendices?   When designed effectively, appendices will increase the usability of your business report. You can avoid bogging down the reader with extremely complex illustrations, lengthy presentations of research data, or preliminary documents (such as the proposal) by moving these items to the back and then referring the interested reader to the proper appendix. By moving such data to the back, you can keep the body of your report lively and concise, thereby decreasing the chances that your reader will set the report down out of boredom or even frustration.

A well-designed set of appendices will present each reader with a choice. If a reader wants more information, that person can follow the textual citation to the appendix in the back and continue reading about a particular subject. If the reader wants only limited information, that person can read the body of the report until satisfied and then move on to the next point. Providing the reader with such a clear set of choices is likely to reflect positively on you as a writer.

What should be included in an appendix?   There really are no hard-and-fast rules on what you can or cannot include. The following items could easily be included as appendices to your report:

- Detailed financial statements, spread sheets, or research data and results
- Complex flow charts or graphic displays
- Preliminary project documents such as a copy of the proposal or progress reports
- Detailed descriptions of your research methodology
- Questionnaires and copies of research tools
- Additional references
- Relevant correspondence

How are appendices sequenced?   Business reports will commonly have more than one appendix, and these appendices should be sequenced in the order that they are referenced in the text. Commonly, each appendix will be titled with a capital letter (e.g., Appendix A: Applications for FCC Licensure). Finally, make certain your table of contents lists the title of each appendix you have included at the end of your report.

2. Document sources in your bibliography

How does a reader locate a specific idea stated in your report? Where might another reader go to learn more about your approach to using focus groups? What about the reader who wants to learn more about the valuation model you relied upon? You can enable your readers to answer these questions, and many more, simply by including text citations in the body of your report (discussed on pages 62–64) along with a bibliography.

What is a bibliography?   A bibliography is simply a list of references and sources that you relied on when initiating the project, conducting the research, or drafting the report. A wide selection of style guides is available to help you create your bibliography. Unless your profession or company has specific style expectations, it probably does not matter which style guide you use. The critical issue is that you construct your bibliography in such a way that you give credit to other people for their ideas and influence, and that you make it easy for the reader to locate and reference the sources you used.

How are bibliographies constructed?   The following is a brief list of some of the most popular style guides. Before buying a style guide, you should speak with knowledgeable colleagues who know if your profession has its own guide. If it does not, any one of the following guides will be useful.

- *Guide to Managerial Communication* by Mary Munter (Prentice Hall)
- *The Chicago Manual of Style* published by The University of Chicago Press
- *The MLA Handbook for Writers of Research Papers* published by The Moden Language Association of America
- *Publication Manual of the American Psychological Association* published by the American Psychological Association.
- *The Business Writer's Handbook* by Gerald J. Alred, Charles T. Brusaw, and Walter E. Oliu (Bedford/St. Martin's)
- *A Writer's Reference* by Diana Hacker (Bedford Books)

The report elements discussed here are all strategic tools that help you manage the project process and effectively communicate your information or recommendations. Each element is strategic because it helps you accomplish some task that is important to your audience. The executive summary provides that terse, up-front description of findings and recommendations that facilitates decision making. Direct patterns of organization enable your readers to find your main ideas easily and allow supporting information to follow naturally as evidence. Back-end materials allow you to include additional and relevant information that meets the needs of inquisitive readers who want more information. You can design a powerful and effective message that meets the diverse problem-solving and decision-making needs of your audience by designing your message strategy and wisely using the report elements presented here.

FORMAL REPORTS: FEATURES AND FUNCTIONS

Feature	Function
Front-end materials	Provide key preliminary information so readers can decide whether to and how to read the report
• Transmittal message	• Formally transmits, via memo or letter, the attached report to the chief decision-making readers
• Title page	• Identifies the key contextual information: topic, target readers, writers, and date prepared
• Executive summary	• Presents a self-sufficient, stand-alone summary that highlights the key ideas contained in the report that follows
• Table of contents	• Enables the readers, at a glance, to identify the main topics in the report body; discern the logical connections among topics; and locate specific topics to read selectively
Report body	Presents concrete data and discussion: conclusions, recommendations, and supporting evidence
• Opening	• Introduces the project, e.g., the governing question, goals, constraints, methodology, and preview of the main topics
• Middle	• Presents carefully arranged segments that reveal the logic of the writer's argument and present the report's detailed evidence
• Closing	• Wraps up the discussion by addressing the implicit question, "What now?"
Back-end materials	Provides supplementary information for readers who seek more detailed discussion
• Appendices	• Present material that is less important or too detailed and lengthy to place it within the report body
• Bibliography	• Enables readers to consult your sources to learn more about specific topics you address

CHAPTER 4 OUTLINE

I. ENSURING CLARITY
   1. Writing simple and clear sentences
   2. Aiding decision making with visual elements
   3. Using text citations with your bibliography

II. ENSURING SKIM VALUE
   1. Emphasizing key ideas with informative headings
   2. Emphasizing key ideas with lists
   3. Using neutral space effectively
   4. Selecting a readable font

CHAPTER 4

How to Design a Readable Report

In Chapter 1, we discussed how business reports help professionals manage projects by providing solutions and serving as a record
of events. Essential to accomplishing both goals is an audience
who *reads* your report. Your report will not be effective if the audience
does not read your document and act on ideas or recommendations.
Effective report writers increase the odds of their report being read
and understood by managing message delivery—that is, managing the
report's design. This chapter will focus on two essential qualities of
effective reports, *clarity* and *skim value*. A well-designed report should
be easy to understand, and desired ideas should be easy to access.

I. ENSURING CLARITY

Your report writing process should produce a clear document. A clear report will contain:

- Ideas phrased in a manner that allows the audience to quickly and easily understand your purpose and key points
- Corresponding ideas that illustrate and elaborate on your key points ·
- Textual references that clearly distinguish between your ideas and ideas borrowed from another author

Simply put, clarity helps the audience understand what your ideas are, see ideas illustrated in graphic form, and distinguish between original and borrowed ideas.

I. Writing simple and clear sentences

If a message is clear, the audience should not need to read it more than once merely to understand it. For example, a writer unintentionally illustrated how important it is to be clear. By unintentionally violating the principle of being clear, she subjected to ridicule both herself and the firm for which she worked. In a report, she wrote:

> On the basis of its assessment of the formidable obstacles to viable organization that would continue to confront workers even under a circumstance of legal rights and protections conductive to that end, the task force is persuaded that collective bargaining is unlikely to become a basis for labor relations or to afford an effective means by which employees might advance their interests.

A New York bank unwittingly became party to a lawsuit requiring plain English in public documents, when it used a 121-word sentence in its rules on safe-deposit boxes.

> The liability of the bank is expressly limited to the exercise of ordinary diligence and care to prevent the opening of the within-mentioned safe-deposit box during the within-mentioned term, or any extension or renewal thereof, by any person other than the lessee or his duly authorized representative and failure to exercise such diligence or care shall

not be inferable from any alleged loss, absence or disappearance or any of its contents, nor shall the bank be liable for permitting a co-lessee or an attorney in fact of the lessee to have access to and remove contents of said safe-deposit box after the lessee's death or disability and before the bank has written knowledge of such death or disability.

In both examples, are the ideas easy to understand? Your response may approximate that of the New York State Attorney General who, after reading the passage in the second example, remarked, "I defy anyone, lawyer or lay person, to understand what that means."

If you want to improve the clarity of your sentences, see Mary Munter's *Guide to Managerial Communication* or the classic *Elements of Style* by Strunk and White.

2. Aiding decision making with visual elements

In addition to improving your sentences, you can also focus on cor-responding and illustrating ideas that support your key points or recommendations. A clear report will have an obvious idea or rec-ommendation that is supported and substantiated by ideas and numeric data. Commonly, these supporting ideas and data are placed in tables, graphs, charts, or figures that have the power to present large bodies of data and demonstrate relationships in a very small space. Effective visual communication allows you to *show* your read-ers important information and relationships. Often, you can show an idea far more easily than you can explain it with text.

Edward Tufte presents several guidelines for effective visual communication in his book *The Visual Display of Quantitative Infor-mation*.

- Use tables to compare two or more specific data points. Tables are commonly limited to 20 data points or fewer, though some larger and more complex tables can be very effective.
- Use graphs to display large data sets and to compare two or more large data sets.
- Use charts when you want to show workflows or processes. Charts can also effectively demonstrate cause and effect (i.e., the measured data on the *x-axis* change value when data on the *y-axis* change value).

The table on the facing page illustrates how visual frameworks can be used in your reports.

Visual communication is most effective when it shows relationships. Communicators worried about clarity will understand the critical relationships in a given project and will find a way to display those relationships visually.

- Can you use a graphic display to show how a production plant has significantly fewer quality control concerns, and thus lower costs, when employees work 10 hours or fewer of overtime each week?

- Can you visually show your reader that an annual employee turnover rate of 20 percent is actually good, compared to the industry standard of 33 percent?

- Can you demonstrate that selling off more than 1.2 million shares of a given stock in a single day will likely drive the price down by as much as 7 percent?

Good visual communication will highlight, or make obvious, changes in information. In other words, visual communication can help make your point clear. Clarity, from our perspective, seems to be one of the critical points that Tufte makes throughout his book. As report writers, you must understand how to make supporting ideas clear so that decision-making and problem-solving audiences can easily follow your arguments.

3. Using text citations with your bibliography

Clearly distinguishing between original and borrowed ideas is a third and final way in which report writers must think about clarity. You want your readers to be clear about which ideas are yours and which are borrowed. For example, say a reader wants to know where you acquired information about emotional intelligence. You can indicate the source of that information by citing the author in the text and including a matching reference in the bibliography.

Together, the text citation and the bibliographic reference indicate where an idea comes from and tell the reader how to locate that information. Textual citations can have the added benefit of potentially increasing your credibility by consistently showing that you have researched your topic and integrated a wide range of ideas and models into your final report. Making your citations usable, however, is of

POSSIBLE VISUAL FRAMEWORKS

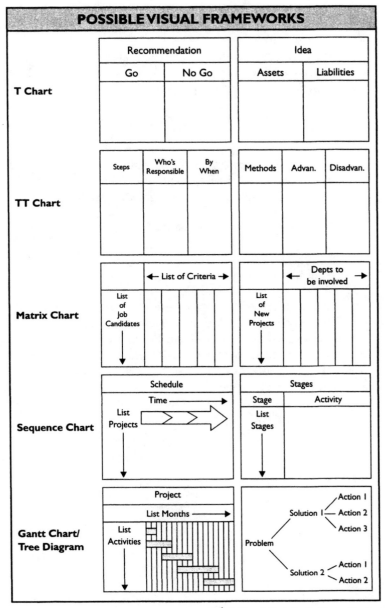

Adapted from J. Howell, *Tools for Facilitating Meetings*

primary importance. You have designed your textual references well if the reader is able to quickly and easily find the full source citation in the bibliography.

The first step in creating a complete textual citation is referencing the source at the end of sentence. The following example shows a textual citation on emotional intelligence:

> ". . . was first introduced in the *Harvard Business Review* (Goleman, 1998)."

The textual reference to Goleman indicates to your readers that a complete source citation can be found elsewhere in the bibliography. A matching bibliographic reference might look like this:

> Goleman, Daniel (1998). What Makes a Leader? *Harvard Busines Review,* 76(6), 92–102.
>
> Hill, Linda A. (1992). *Becoming a Manager: Mastery of a New Identity.* Boston: Harvard Business School Publishing, p. 57.

Note how the bibliographic reference uses a hanging indention. The second line is indented while the first is left justified. This is another example of how you can increase the usability of your document. The reader is able to easily and quickly skim down the list of names and locate a specific reference because neutral or white space surrounds the names. If all the text were left justified, the names would be difficult to separate from the full citation, thereby decreasing usability.

II. ENSURING SKIM VALUE

Early in Chapter 1 we suggested that business professionals commonly do not read reports the way some people might read an essay or work of literature. What this means is that businesspeople are often too busy to read a report word for word from start to finish. In fact, the only part of your report that you can assume the audience will read carefully is the executive summary. Readers are more likely to read your report if key ideas are easy to find and if your document is quick and easy to move through.

Effective business writers focus on skim value. They emphasize their key ideas by using: (1) informative headings, (2) lists, (3) neutral space, and (4) readable font.

I. Emphasizing key ideas with informative headings

Effective headings will allow the reader to glance at a page and immediately recognize the key idea presented in that segment of the report. Effective headings:

- Increase skim value by setting off key ideas through visual variety (e.g., boldface, large font size, etc.).
- Break the report into manageable or "bite-size" sections.
- Increase audience comprehension by placing meaningful ideas or recommendations at the heading level.

For example, your report readers may wonder, "How does this affect our department?" or "What staffing changes do I need to make as a result of this policy?" Subtopic questions like these, or the general answer to such questions, can sometimes be stated in your headings, where they will be most obvious. By placing your subtopic question or general answer to a question in your headings, you can help the reader quickly skim a report for main ideas, comprehend the main idea of each section, and interpret a section's specific data within the light of a main idea.

Helping your audience comprehend main ideas and their relationship to supporting data is particularly important. It is virtually impossible for readers to understand how specific pieces of concrete data or supporting information fit together if they do not *first* understand the answer you are providing to a subtopic question. The organizational pattern where we first provide an answer to a subtopic question, and second provide the data or support for that answer, is called a *direct pattern of organization.* Business readers with an eye toward action will commonly appreciate a direct pattern of organization.

Therefore, push your answers to subtopic questions, or the questions themselves, up to the heading level whenever possible. Additionally, craft informative headings and use an active verb. Headings that lack an active verb present your readers with only a topic. An active verb such as *finance, hire,* or *organize* will speak to the decision maker's action and immediately indicate what needs to be done.

The following examples illustrate the difference between topical and informative headings. The first list illustrates topical headings that provide only topics and tell the reader little about the actual ideas being presented.

- Opening
- Problem
- Recommendation One
- Recommendation Two
- Recommendation Three
- Conclusion

Now, consider the following list of informative headings. Note how the sequence of informative headings forms a narrative flow.

- Why are we losing market share to our competition?
- Should we be concerned about customer loyalty?
- Should we form alliances to improve our competitive position?
- Should we increase our ad expenditures in target markets?
- Can we set 28 percent as our target market share?

The difference between topical and informative headings should be immediately obvious. The informative headings give a clear narrative flow to your report and increase the readers' ability to skim important ideas. Your document will also have increased usability. Readers can flip through your report and easily find desired ideas and explanations. Finally, your report will have greater visual variety because ideas are broken down into smaller segments and because headings are set off by white space (discussed later in this chapter) and variations in font.

In short, effective headings can secure a tremendously positive impact on your readers' ability to skim a report and on their perception of your credibility. Use headings to your advantage.

2. Emphasizing key ideas with lists

Lists are a second feature for improving your reader's ability to skim your report. Lists help you emphasize ideas and draw the readers' attention to a certain portion of the page. If you have a series of ideas that deserve special attention, you might consider presenting them in a list format.

Types of lists   Lists can be of two types: bulleted and enumerated. Both types of lists are typically indented on the left and aligned vertically. Bulleted lists are typically used to present a set of related ideas that are not in a particular or sequential order. Enumerated lists are used to present your ideas in series when sequence is especially important.

Parallelism in lists   You can increase the readers' ability to skim a list by constructing each item with parallel phrasing. Parallel phrasing simply means that similar ideas are presented in a grammatically similar form. For example, all items in your list should begin with an active verb if the first item begins with an active verb. The same rule would apply if the first item in your list started with a noun. All items in the list, then, would start with a noun.

In the example below, can you see how each item begins with an active verb? This is what we mean by parallel structure. Parallel structure helps the reader skim your report and quickly grasp key ideas that you are setting apart in the list.

- Present similar ideas in a similar fashion.

- Begin all items with the same part of speech (e.g., begin each item with a verb or begin each item with a noun).

- Use enumeration if the ideas are in a ranked or sequential order.

3. Using neutral space effectively

Neutral space, also known as white space, can be a powerful tool for creating visually inviting documents that are easy to skim. Neutral space refers to the empty or unused space on a page that provides visual breathing room to the reader's eye. Neutral space can help you break your document into portions that are manageable for the reader, highlight important ideas such as lists or headings, indicate breaks in the information flow, and improve readability.

Managing portions   Many business readers will want the option to move quickly through a document if they choose. Therefore, your document design must allow for effective skimming. Long, drawn-out paragraphs that fill a page side to side and top to bottom do not encourage skimming. Long paragraphs instead require reading. Many readers who wish to skim will simply skip over long paragraphs or ask you for the main idea rather than take the time to read it. In this one sense, then, documents designed for detailed, chronological reading will often not allow for skimming.

Documents designed for skimming, on the other hand, do not rule out the possibility of reading. Rather than writing one very long paragraph that fills an entire page or more, break the long paragraph into shorter paragraphs and separate each with neutral space. A series of short paragraphs will enhance the audience's ability to skim while in no way eliminating the possibility of reading your report word for word. Reports designed with short paragraphs visually separated by white space will accommodate both types of readers.

Highlighting ideas   Key ideas can be set off and given additional emphasis by surrounding them with white space. Lists, for example, provide additional neutral space between the bullet and the text. Lists are also typically surrounded with a visual frame of neutral space. The additional neutral space helps the list to stand out and appear obvious to the reader. The strict alignment of text provides a clear line for the reader's eye to follow. The combined effect is strong visual emphasis or highlighting of the list.

Indicating breaks   Neutral space can also be used to indicate breaks in the information flow. Take a moment and think about the last book you read. Did you notice that a chapter ending might be followed by a large amount of neutral space at the bottom of the page or even by a blank page? Did you notice that the chapter number or title was surrounded by extremely large amounts of neutral space? Chapter endings and beginnings are good examples of how large amounts of neutral space can be used to indicate breaks in the flow of information. On a smaller scale, neutral space surrounding internal chapter or unit headings indicate smaller breaks in the information flow. Much like a transition, neutral space can subtly indicate that you are moving on to a different topic and that the reader should be mentally prepared for the change.

Improving readability   You should generally use a ragged right margin rather than justifying both sides of your text. Justified margins will frequently increase the neutral space between words and letters rather than allowing neutral space to form a visual frame *around* your text. Additionally, the uneven spacing can increase strain on the reader's eye and reduce readability. As a rule of thumb, your report will be more user friendly if you leave all the neutral space at the end of a line rather than dividing it up between letters and words.

4. Selecting a readable font

Font choice is the final issue related to skim value. A good font choice will make your document easy to read. The audience will rarely, if ever, have to strain their eyes to see what is printed on the page. Some experts have devoted a considerable part of their professional lives to understanding font design and readability. From these experts we can learn two basic rules.

Use serif fonts for paper documents.

For paper documents, choose a serif font such as one of the following:

Times New Roman or Garamond

Serif fonts work extremely well on paper with its high-resolution capabilities. The quality of today's inkjet and laser printers is so high that serif fonts reproduce extremely well and can dramatically increase the readability of your report. The artistic and curled letter ends of serif fonts can reduce eyestrain and positively impact readability. As a rule of thumb, use a serif font for the body of nearly all documents printed on paper.

Use sans-serif fonts for electronic documents.

If your document will be read electronically, choose a sans-serif font, such as either of the following:

Ariel or Helvetica

The pixel design of computer screens and projectors gives the visual image a relatively low resolution. Serif fonts, with their artistic and curled letter ends, commonly do not show up well on the computer or projector screens. The pixels simply are not always able to reproduce such fine detail. The end result may be lettering that has obvious gaps and reduced readability. You can avoid these gaps and increase your document's readability by using a sans serif font.

Combine fonts under certain circumstances

Many writers like to increase the contrast between headings and text by using sans serif font for the headings and using serif fonts for the text. This book is a good example of that style. Have you noticed how the major headings use a font that does not have artistic or curled letter ends? You can increase the visual variety of your reports, and the contrast between headings and text, by using sans serif fonts for the headings and a serif font for the text.

Delivering an effective business report requires that you think about clarity and skim value. This chapter has provided you with seven tools for increasing both of these important report qualities.

- Achieve clarity through simple and clear sentences, visual elements, and text citations that match your bibliography.
- Assure skim value by using informative headings, lists, neutral space, and readable fonts.

Effective report delivery relies on these techniques, which should become an integral part of your message design or strategy. Some elements, such as informative headings, can improve clarity and skim value. Other elements, such as font choice, primarily impact only skim value. Regardless of impact, the techniques discussed in this chapter are ideal tools for designing an easy-to-use report that positively impacts perceptions of your credibility.

APPENDIX: EXAMPLES

I. TRANSMITTAL DOCUMENT

II. EXECUTIVE SUMMARY

III. TITLE PAGE

IV. TABLE OF CONTENTS

Appendix I: Example Transmittal Document

<table>
<tr>
<td>

COGENT
</td>
<td>

123 E. LANSING STREET
MIDDLETON, NH 12345
(123) 456-7890
</td>
</tr>
</table>

October 24, 2001

Ms. Carolyn J. Polanski
Fabrico Manufacturing
22 Buffalo Court
Troy, Ohio 45333

Dear Ms. Polanski:

As you requested in our July 10 consulting agreement, we have assessed the inventory management and communication processes at your Covington plant.

Our analysis reveals three primary opportunities for increasing profitability. If you take advantage of these opportunities, you should be able to fully utilize staff and assets to deliver "the right part at the right place at the right time." Our recommendations will address the following:

- *Inventory levels.* Improved management of your inventory levels will enable you to free assets that are currently being tied-up in high inventory levels.

- *Employee involvement with external stakeholders.* Fabrico could improve its communication with vendors, shipping companies, and sister plants. Improved external communications may also improve internal work processes.

- *Seamless communication across the internal supply chain.* Improved internal procedures could encourage employees to identify process improvements and enhance communication practices.

Most of the information contained in this report was generated through management and staff interviews. These interviews would not have been possible without the direct support and leadership of Jorge Martinez, Vice President of Operations. Additionally, we appreciate the assistance of Sheryl Roever, John Holt, J.B. Bicken, and Carl Orn. Finally, we would like to thank employees at your Covington facility who spoke with us, answered questions, and tolerated our observations.

Thank you for the opportunity to work on this project. We hope our research yields improvements and increases overall profitability of Fabrico Manufacturing. If you have any questions about the report, please call me directly at (123) 456-5432.

Cordially,

Josh Black
Partner

Executive Summary

As you know, Fabrico Manufacturing aims to be the dominant North American provider of welding parts and supplies by providing "the right part at the right time." In its effort to become a top supplier, Fabrico has requested that COGENT, Inc., analyze internal operations and recommend specific strategies for improving the Covington facility's role in the supply chain.

After two months of conducting interviews and focus groups and shadowing staff at the Covington facility, COGENT believes that Fabrico is not optimizing its inventory due to inadequate communication, both within and external to the Covington facility.

Specifically, COGENT makes the following three recommendations.

- *Reevaluate inventory levels.* Manage inventory levels by distinguishing between high and low demand parts or materials. Improved inventory management should reduce inventory costs but will be dependent on Fabrico's ability to effectively gather and share information.

- *Increase employee involvement with internal and external stakeholders.* Headquarters, distributors, and sister plants should begin talking directly with one another. A direct model of communication should help everyone understand needs, implement process improvements, and achieve buy-in regarding changes. Effective communication should also help the plant assess demand and reduce its inventory of low-volume materials.

- *Promote seamless communication across the internal supply chain.* Charge a best practices committee with overseeing and implementing internal improvements that will help create a culture where employees achieve seamless internal communication. Fabrico's Covington facility should become more profitable if information flows freely between internal and external stakeholders—thereby allowing an efficient supply chain to reduce the need for costly inventories.

Implementing these policies should help ensure that Fabrico delivers "the right part is at the right place at the right time."

**Improving Inventory Levels
and Communication Channels
at Fabrico Manufacturing's
Covington Facility**

Prepared for

Ms. Carolyn J. Polanski
Fabrico Manufacturing
Troy, Ohio 45333

Presented by

Josh Black, Partner
COGENT, Inc.
Middleton, NH 12345

October 24, 2001

Table of Contents

BIBLIOGRAPHY

This bibliography provides a very select listing of books for further reference and serves to acknowledge the sources noted in the book.

Alred, G., C. Brusaw, and W.E. Oliu, *The Business Writer's Handbook,* 6th ed. Boston: Bedford/St. Martin, 2000.

Gibaldi, J., *MLA Handbook for Writers of Research Papers,* 5th ed. The Modern Language Association of America, New York, 1999.

Grossman, J., *The Chicago Manual of Style: The Essential Guide for Writers, Editors, and Publishers.* The University of Chicago Press, 1993.

Hacker, D., *A Writer's Reference,* 4th ed. Bedford Books, 1999.

Halpern, J., J. Kilborn, and A. Lokke, *Business Writing Strategies and Samples.* New York: Macmillan Publishing Company, 1988.

Howell, J., *Tools for Facilitating Meetings.* Seattle: Integrity Publishing, 1995.

Lanham, R., *Revising Business Prose,* 4th ed. Allyn & Bacon, 2000.

Minto, B., *The Pyramid Principle: Logic in Writing, Thinking, and Problem Solving.* London: Minto International, Inc., 1995.

Munter, M., *Guide to Managerial Communication: Effective Business Writing and Speaking,* 5th ed. Upper Saddle River, NJ: Prentice Hall, 2000.

Securities Exchange Commission. Office of Investor Education and Assistance. *A Plain English Handbook: How to Create Clear SEC Disclosure Documents.* Washington: GPO, 1998.

Strunk, W. and E. White, *The Elements of Style,* 4th ed. Allyn & Bacon, 2000.

The American Psychological Association. *Publication Manual of the American Psychological Association.* Washington, DC, 2000.

Tufte, E., *The Visual Display of Quantitative Information.* Cheshire, CT: Graphics Press, 1992.

Williams, J., *Style: Ten Lessons in Clarity and Grace,* 6th ed. Chicago: Addison Wesley Longman, Inc., 2000.

Zelazny, G., *Say It With Charts: The Executive's Guide to Visual Communication,* 3rd ed. Homewood, IL: Dow Jones-Irwin, 1996.

Index

Page numbers followed by f indicate figure. Pages numbers followed by t indicate table.